STITCHERY • FIRST BOOK

Through special arrangement with
Whitman Publishing Company—Racine, Wisconsin

WHITMAN JUVENILES

are now available to schools and libraries in

GOLDENCRAFT BINDING

from

GOLDEN PRESS, INC.

Educational Division

850 Third Avenue—New York 22, N. Y.

Stitchery

Long ago, people in Asia, Europe, and in other lands used colored threads stitched in patterns to decorate furniture coverings, clothing, and other fabrics that they used from day to day. They also made large fabric pictures known as banners. Today we call such decorative embroidery *stitchery* art. This book shows you how to make the basic stitches that those people invented and used. You can use these stitches to decorate place mats and other fabrics, and to make toys and banners. And then you can learn to "draw" with your needle and thread, invent your own stitches, and make your own stitchery pictures and designs!

For stitchery projects you need only household supplies: a ruler, scissors, pins, sewing needles, fabrics, and thread. The best stitchery fabrics are loosely woven materials: burlap, linen, and heavy cotton or wool. Beginners will find that it is easiest to work with inexpensive burlap, which can be bought in a variety of colors. Other unusual background materials that you will want to experiment with are wire mesh, plastic foam, paper, and oilcloth. For your thread, collect sewing and darning threads, twine, knitting and weaving yarn, colored string, and metallic threads. You can even use unraveled yarn from old sweaters! Sort out odds and ends of thread by color and store them in plastic bags. Save a special container for wooden beads, buttons, wire, rickrack, pieces of suede, net, lace, and other decorative materials to add to your stitchery art.

The children participating in these activities are students in the Wilmette Public Schools, Wilmette, Illinois.
Photographs by Egons Tomsons

© Copyright 1967 by Western Publishing Company, Inc.
WHITMAN PUBLISHING COMPANY
Racine, Wisconsin

Printed in the U.S.A.

scissors, needles

hread

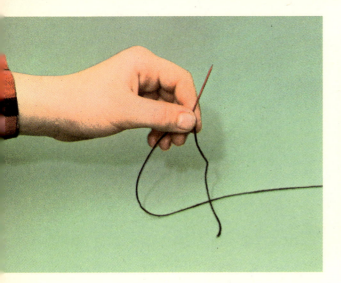 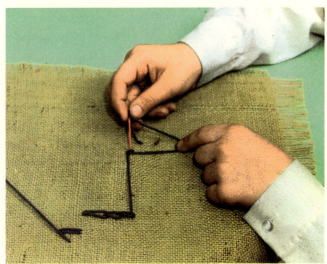

There are several kinds of scissors that are helpful to have. Pinking shears can be used to cut a zigzag edge on fabrics. Embroidery or manicure scissors are good for working with fine threads. When you cut cloth, open the scissors and cut so that the cloth is all the way in to where the two blades come together.

Darning needles or sewing needles with large "eyes" (openings in the needles through which the threads are pulled) are easy to thread. Family sewing supplies usually include a needle-threading tool which can also be used. After the needle is threaded, tie a knot at one end of the thread. You can also pull the two ends until they are even, tie them together, and work with a double thread.

There are many thread materials that you can use for stitchery, even fishing line and kite string can be used, but at first you will prefer to work with heavy yarn and a tapestry or darning needle.

You will also need cloth that has a "loose weave." This means that there are open spaces between the threads that make up the cloth, and heavy yarn can be stitched through these openings. Later on you can work with smaller threads and finely woven materials.

Now you are ready to try the stitch designs on the next pages. Make a *stitchery sampler* — a square piece of cloth with a sample of each stitch that you learn to make. It isn't necessary to cut and knot your yarn after making each different stitch design. Just bring the needle up through another part of the fabric and begin another stitch.

running stitch

These first stitches could be called "line-making" stitches. You can use these stitches to make stitchery outlines or line designs. The running stitch is the easiest of all stitches. Move the needle and thread in and out of the cloth to make a row of stitches. Try long stitches or small stitches. If your needle has a large eye, thread it with two threads of different colors and make double running stitches.

cross-stitch

Bring the needle up through the cloth and begin a row of even, slanting stitches. To produce a row of cross-stitches, sew back over the stitches, crossing each slanted diagonal stitch with a stitch of equal length slanting in the opposite direction. You can make a line with a small row of cross-stitches or fill in a large area with big cross-stitching.

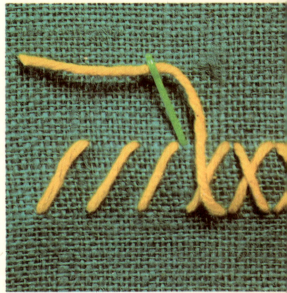

couching

Arrange a single strand or several strands of string or yarn on the cloth. Push the needle up through your fabric and bring it out next to the string or yarn. Stitch directly across this until it is securely attached. Use couching stitches to fasten twigs, straws, strings of beads, and other similar materials to fabric.

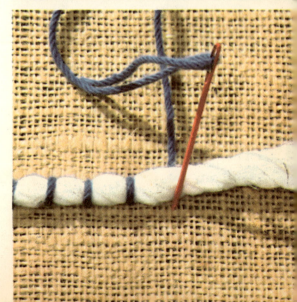

titches

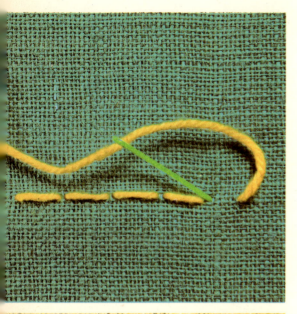

backstitch

Make a short stitch, pushing the needle and thread down into your fabric. Bring the needle up through the cloth a short distance ahead of the first stitch. Make a stitch *back* to your original stitch so the thread covers the open area of cloth, again bringing the thread up through the material a short distance beyond the end of the last stitch. Repeat to form a continuous line of stitches.

blanket stitch

Push the needle up through the fabric. Make a loop and hold it down with your thumb, inserting the needle to the right and down through the material. Bring the needle up through the fabric within this thread loop so that it is caught and held to one side, then form another loop. Continue by working the needle in and then out over the looped threads.

outline stitch

Make backstitches, slanting and overlapping each stitch so that it appears to curve around the next stitch. The outline stitch and the backstitch can both be used to form curved and straight lines and to outline shapes in stitchery designs.

more stitches

french knot

Bring the needle up and wrap thread around it two or three times. Insert the needle next to where the thread was pulled through. Push the needle through to the other side of the fabric, holding the knot in place until you have tightened your thread.

bundle stitch

Make four or five straight stitches close to each other. Bring the needle up through the cloth beneath the stitches and wrap your thread around the strands several times. Insert your needle back into the cloth.

seed stitch

Make two short stitches with a single or double thread. These tiny stitches can be made in any direction and used to fill in shapes or background areas.

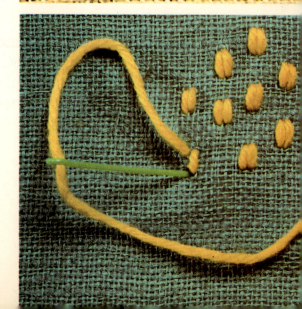

The stitches on these pages are "fill-in" stitches because they can be used for filling in open areas or stitchery shapes. After you have added fill-in stitches to the line-making stitches on your sampler, change them and invent your own stitchery patterns. Three rows of running stitches curve around chain stitching to make this design. How do you think the "bow" of loose threads was made?

chain stitch

Work the needle up through the cloth; make a loop with the thread and hold it with your thumb. Insert the needle next to where the thread was pulled up through the fabric. Bring the needle back up through the cloth and over the looped thread so that the loop is caught by the strand of thread. Make a loop with this thread, insert the needle in through the cloth within the first loop, and then up again so that this loop is caught.

satin stitch

Make a straight stitch. Add more stitches next to your first thread until you have filled in a solid area of fabric with smooth stitches. Change the stitch lengths to form and fill in circles, squares, triangles, and other shapes.

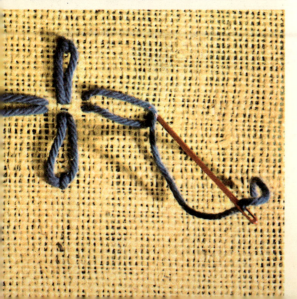

lazy daisy stitch

Make single chain stitches and hold each loop of thread in place with a tiny stitch. Center the thread loops to form stitchery flower petals.

easy weaving

Materials: *wire mesh, frame materials, liquid starch, tape, scissors, rug yarn, knitting yarn, ribbons, shoelaces, and natural weaving materials such as rag strips, twine, grass, and string.*

This is a good project for beginners. Even very young artists can "weave" with ribbons and thick yarn. Cut a square piece of wire mesh; to make the mesh sturdier and easier to handle, tack or staple it to an old picture frame or a frame cut from a piece of cardboard. Apply liquid starch to one end of the yarn strands, making the tip of your yarn as stiff as a needle. Ribbon ends can be curled into a point and wrapped with tape so that they are easier to weave with.

Now guide the yarn or ribbon under and over the mesh strands. As you weave, can you guess what stitch you are making? The *running stitch!* So you see, it isn't necessary to know all kinds of stitches in order to make a stitchery design. Choose other yarns and ribbons in colors that you like and build colorful patterns. Look around for colored strings and other unusual materials to add to your weaving. For summertime fun, try weaving with grasses, reeds, and dandelion stems!

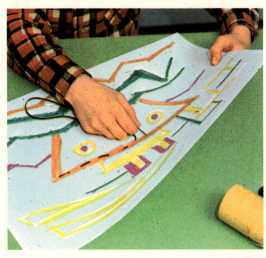
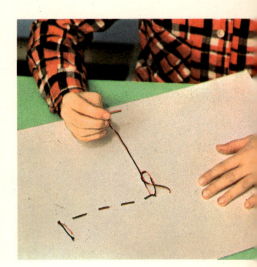

1   2

You need: *heavy drawing paper, crayons, a large needle, scissors, and yarn or colored string.*

Make a simple crayon drawing on a sheet of white or manila drawing paper or colored construction paper. Thread a large needle with a piece of yarn no more than two feet long. (A longer length can become tangled as you work.) Pull this thread through the needle so that about five inches of string or yarn extends down on one side. Tie a knot at the other end.

With the point of your needle, push a small hole in the paper through one of the lines in your drawing. Hold the threaded needle underneath the drawing paper and bring the needle up through the hole that you have made. Do this so that the knotted end of the thread will

be on the other side of the paper. Whether you stitch on paper or on fabric, it is best to start your stitchery this way.

Cover the lines in your drawing with lines of stitches. Practice the running stitch; make long stitches, then small, even ones. Perhaps you will overlap all the lines with running stitches, or you might want to try the backstitch or the outline stitch. You can add fill-in stitches within the shapes and open areas in your drawing. To finish your crayon and thread picture, tie the thread in a knot on the back of the paper sheet and cut away the extra thread.

Another thread picture to try: "draw" with your needle and thread and invent your own stitches, building a picture out of them on a plain piece of paper.

thread picture

balloon

1

2

fish

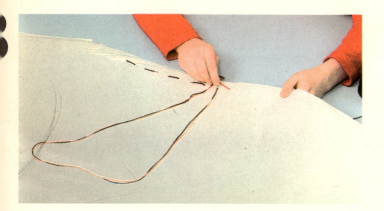

Materials: *large sheets of paper (brown wrapping paper is fine), a large needle, yarn or colored string, scissors, tape, newspapers, and painting materials.*

Bulging "balloon fish" are as fun and easy to make as they look! Draw the outline of a fish on a large sheet of paper. Slide a second piece of paper under the first piece and tape the two sheets together. Using your drawing as a guide, cut the fish form out of both sheets of paper at the same time. Arrange the two cutout shapes, one on top of the other, so that they match perfectly, and use tape or paper clips to hold them in place. Thread a large needle with yarn or a double strand of colored string. Start a short distance in from the edge of your fish and stitch around most of the two paper shapes. Leave one end open for padding. Crumple newspapers and stuff your paper figure with them. Then stitch the remaining open edges together.

Decorate your balloon fish with bright poster paint colors and hang it from the ceiling. You can make other balloon shapes (a pig, butterflies, an airplane, funny people, prehistoric creatures) and use them as mobiles, toys, or bulletin board decorations.

Look for: *papers (heavy drawing paper, wax paper, gift wrap, corrugated cardboard, colored papers), scissors, straight pins, a large needle, and string or thread.*

"Appliqué" is another form of stitchery art. Appliqués are cloth shapes cut from one fabric and sewn or glued onto another material. You can learn to make appliqué designs with paper cutouts.

Cut out paper shapes. Use pinking shears, if you own them, to trim around some of your shapes. Tear, pleat, and crumple other paper forms, placing smaller pieces on top of larger shapes. After you have arranged the shapes on a piece of heavy paper, pin them down with straight pins. Thread a large needle with thread or string and stitch the paper cutouts in place. You can stitch around the edge of the paper shapes with a running stitch or make French knots and cross-stitches in the center of the paper cutouts. When your paper forms are securely held, remove the straight pins.

appliqué

1

2

3

1

Materials: *ribbons, yarn, or other string materials used for "easy weaving," a rug or darning needle, tape, liquid starch, scissors, and burlap, mesh vegetable sacks, or loosely woven plastic mesh.*

Cut a large piece of material from a mesh vegetable sack for potatoes, onions, or oranges. Or use a mesh dishcloth, or pull out threads from a piece of burlap to make an open-weave fabric. Some yarns can be threaded through a large needle; to weave with ribbon or string, stiffen the ends by taping them or dipping them in liquid starch.

Weave in and out of the mesh fibers with large, loose stitches, leaving open spaces in your design. Make up your own stitches to form new patterns. Allow the yarns to twist around each other and hang from the fabric. When you hold your stitchery up, you should be able to see through it.

2

Display your stitchery design on a brightly colored fabric or paper, or hang it in front of a window. For a family project, stitch several "see through" designs together, mount them on a frame, and use this as a room divider.

weaving

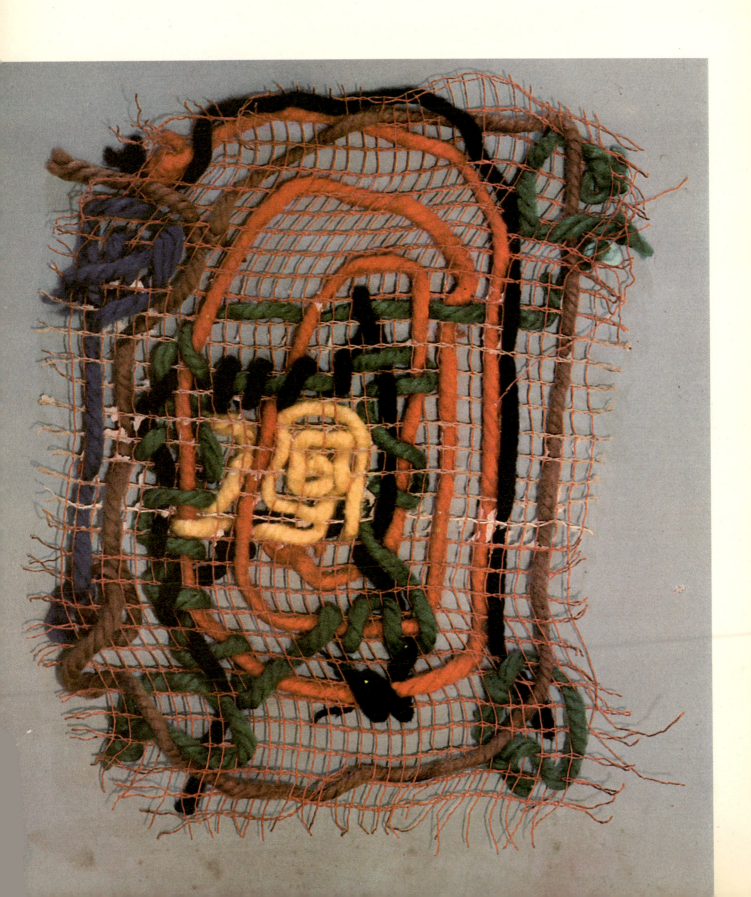

You need: *burlap, other fabric scraps, threads, yarns, needles, scissors, paper, a pencil, and straight pins. If your fabric is wrinkled, press it with a warm iron.*

Burlap fringes are easy to make. First, cut the selvage off of the burlap. "Selvage" is a special woven edge that does not look like the rest of the material. This woven edge prevents the rest of the fabric from unraveling. Now pull away threads along the four outside edges — and you will have a fringe. You can fringe almost any loosely woven fabric. Save the extra threads that you have pulled out for other stitchery projects.

Cloth appliqués can be cut out directly, but for some projects you might want to plan your appliqués in advance. Here is how to do this. Start with paper appliqués; cut paper shapes and arrange them, then use the paper shapes as patterns. Pin each shape to a fabric and cut around it through the cloth to make a cloth appliqué. Pin the cloth appliqués down and stitch them. If you want your stitches to show as part of your design, choose colored threads that differ from the color of the cloth. These are called "contrasting colors."

It's fun to try felt, silk, velvet, and other materials when you appliqué. For a beginning activity, however, you will want to use fabric, like burlap, that is easily cut and sewn. For this first "fringe and appliqué" project, each appliqué was fringed before it was sewn to the burlap backing. The design was completed with imaginative stitchery.

1   **2**

3

4

anima

1

2

Materials: *heavy yarn or cotton cording, thread, needles, straight pins, scissors, white glue, tape, fabric scraps, and burlap.*

Let's make animal banners! These colorful cloth pictures begin with a couching design. Spread a large piece of fringed or plain burlap or some other heavy backing material out on your work area. Drop a length of heavy yarn or cotton cord onto this fabric and poke and push it until you form the outline of an animal. You can add other pieces of yarn and cloth appliqués, temporarily pinning them in position. Thread a needle and carefully work it under the burlap back-

ground until the point of the needle is just under your yarn design. Bring the needle up through the fabric next to the yarn and hold the yarn in place with couching stitches.

Fill in open areas in your design with cloth shapes, strings, fluffy yarn, and other decorative materials. Use stitching or household glue to hold these materials in place. Finish an unfringed burlap banner by folding the rough edges underneath and taping them to the back of the design. To hang your banner, fold over the top edge of the fabric and glue or stitch it down in back. Insert a wooden dowel, a garden stake, or a long stick through this fold and tie yarn to the two ends.

banners

3

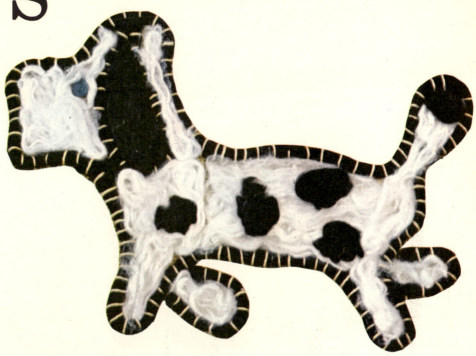

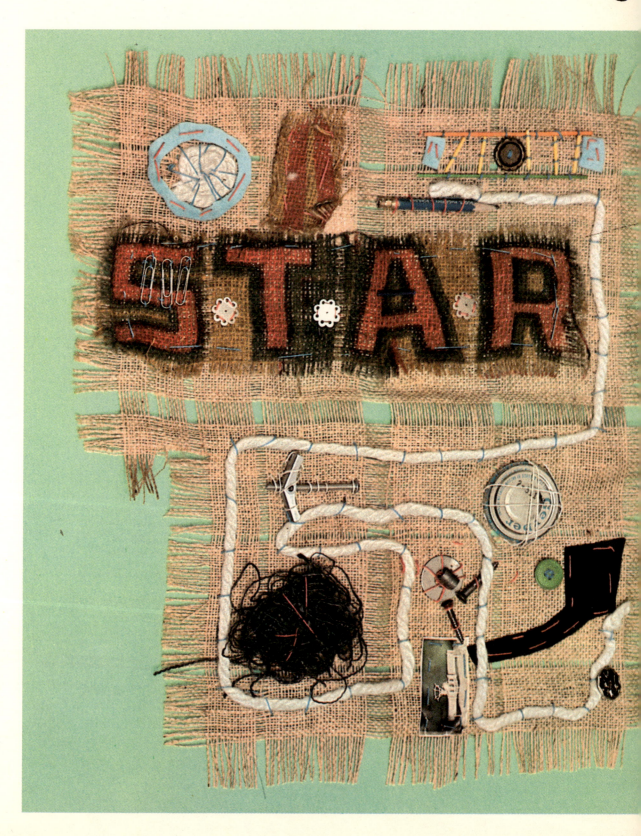

nd found objects

You need: *burlap or other backing fabric, scissors, sewing needles, string or heavy threads, white glue, and "found" materials.*

Find all kinds of objects and materials that would be fun to use in a design. They can be unusual items or everyday things. Look for bits of fur, bottle caps, lace, paper clips, costume jewelry, cotton balls, colored sticks, and soda straws. Make a collection of these "found objects"; you can use them for other art projects also.

Cut the selvage from your backing fabric with scissors and pull threads to form a fringe. Arrange an assortment of objects and glue or stitch them in place. You will have to experiment with a variety of stitches to see which type of stitch works best. Large couching stitches or bundle stitching will hold many materials; others can be attached with glue. Make a picture that reminds you of something special. For a "seashore" design, you can add sandpaper, long grass, shiny foil or a mirror for the "sea," and toy fish and sea animals. If you collect seashells when you go to the beach, stitch some of these into your design. You can even create stitchery pictures that are interesting to touch as well as look at. Stitch or glue scraps of fur, leather, soft velvet, and feathers to make a stitchery that *feels* like a "zoo"!

1

2

stitchery

1 **2** **3**

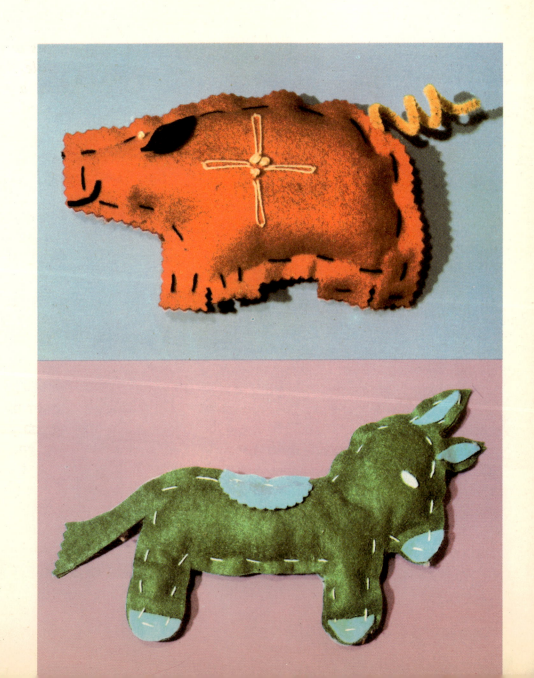

oys

Make a large stitchery "animal pillow" to match your stitchery toy! Foam rubber or mattress stuffing can be used to stuff larger forms.

4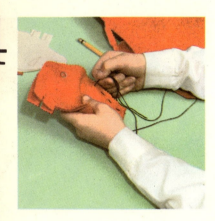

5

Tools and materials: *scissors or pinking shears, straight pins, a needle, thread, glue, a crayon or chalk, paper, a pencil, felt or another sturdy fabric, and cotton.*

Sketch an animal, a flower, a train, or some other toy figure on a piece of paper, then cut it out. This paper shape is the pattern for your fabric toy. Pin the paper pattern to the fabric. Use a piece of chalk or a crayon to draw an outline on fabric around the paper figure and cut out this shape. If you have pinking shears, use them to cut a zigzag edge around the fabric shape. Then make another cloth figure just like the first one.

Arrange the second fabric shape on top of the first and stitch the shapes together with running stitches or blanket stitches. Leave an opening so cotton can be stuffed inside. After you have added the cotton, complete the stitching. Stitchery trimming can be added before the two cloth shapes are sewn together, or you might prefer to cut a "nose," "eyes," and other details from scraps and glue them to your finished figure.

stitchin

n plastic foam

Materials needed: *styrene plastic foam, crayons, tape, a needle, string or thread, and scissors. You can buy sheets of white styrene foam at variety stores and hobby shops.*

Crayon a picture on one side of a piece of plastic foam. (Or glue paper shapes or fabrics in a design.) Thread your needle with colored string or thread; a single or double strand can be used. Tie a knot at the end of the thread and bring the threaded needle up through the foam until most of the thread has been pulled through. Tape the knotted end of the thread to the back of the plastic foam so that the thread will not pull completely through. Now "draw" with your needle and thread and stitch a design over the background shapes. Try this project with threads in a variety of sizes and colors.

1

2

3

4

Materials: *cardboard, tape, string or thread, a pencil, a large needle, and a ruler.*

With a pencil and ruler draw two lines that form an angle on a piece of cardboard. Draw one line longer than the other. The angle you make can be a right angle, or more or less than a right angle. Start at the point where the two lines come together, and on each line mark the same number of evenly spaced dots. The spaces between the dots on the long line will be wider than those you have marked off on the short line. Number the dots 1, 2, 3, and so on, as shown, then make holes through the dot marks with a needle. Thread your needle and start it under the cardboard (tape the thread end down in back). Bring the needle up through hole 1, over and in through hole 2, out at 3, down through 4, out at 5, down through 6, out at 7. Continue doing this until the threading is finished.

designs

This unusual pattern of threads will suggest many picture ideas to you. After you begin with a practice design, plan how to make your own thread picture.